PLAY·THE·GAME

WINDSURFING

Farrel O'Shea

WARD LOCK

First published in 1991
by Ward Lock,
Villiers House, 41/47 Strand, London WC2N 5JE
England.

A Cassell imprint

Illustrations by Tony Randell

Text set in Helvetica
by Chapterhouse Ltd, The Cloisters, Halsall Lane,
Formby, L37 3PX
Printed and bound in Great Britain by Richard
Clay, Bungay

British Library Cataloguing in Publication Data
O'Shea, Farrel
Windsurfing. – (Play the game)
1. Windsurfing
I. Title   II. Series

ISBN 0 7063 6971 8

Acknowledgements

The author and publisher would like to thank Max
Earey, Alex Williams, Buz Sipes and F2
International for supplying photographs.

**Britt Dunkerbeck, sister of Bjorn, is a
competent sailor in the waves and a
leading female competitor.**

CONTENTS

FOREWORD

Ask any windsurfer what attracts him or her to the sport and, suddenly animated, he or she will search vainly to find words to describe the most exhilarating, most liberated sensation on earth. Ask the same person what it was like to learn and improve and they will relate the story of a bitter, (albeit sometimes enjoyable) fight to hop up to the next performance level.

Learning any new skill is hard enough, but when you are asked to do it in an ever-changing environment, the challenge is sometimes formidable. Every day I come across competent performers who are so frustrated by their apparent inability to move on, that they're ready to throw in the towel. Even more frustrating is the fact that windsurfing is in no way difficult, it is just that the necessary guidance is not always at hand; or if it is, it is not readily under-standable.

It is therefore with great pleasure that I introduce and endorse Farrel O'Shea's new book on windsurfing technique. Farrel is that rarest of combinations – a first class performer who can share and communicate his undoubted skill. He is probably the most visually exciting sailor in the country; having sailed with the best sailors in the world, at the windiest, wildest locations in the world, his depth of knowledge is fathomless.

Whereas many authors before him have tried to drown us in a sea of technical mumbo-jumbo, Farrel refuses to blind us with hydro- and aerodynamic science. Instead, in his lucid and amusing style, he concentrates on the meat of the problem – the techniques themselves, offering us snippets of theory only when they help clarify a point. **Play the Game: Windsurfing** will be your indispens-able beachside companion.

Peter Hart
RYA Chief Funboard Trainer

The author enters a forward rotating loop off the Hawaiian shores off Hookipa, Maui.

HISTORY &
DEVELOPMENT OF
WINDSURFING

Within a few short years windsurfing has transformed from an obscure minority sport into perhaps the most popular watersport of the modern era. The sport has no climatic or topographical boundaries – where there is water, there is windsurfing, whether it be the scrubbiest gravel pit or the awesome waves that beat upon the shores of the Hawaiian islands. It is not difficult to see why there are now millions of participants world wide, spanning the five oceans, and the five continents; given some knowledge of the basic concepts one can quickly experience the joys of sailing, coupled with the thrills and spills of surfing.

The origins of windsurfing go back to 1965 when an American, Newman Derby, published what appeared to be a rather eccentric idea in the journal *Popular Science*. Derby's basic principle of the 'freesail' – the idea that the board can be directed by movement of the mast, back and forth – is still valid today.

It was not until much later in the decade that a sailboard more akin to today's craft was seen. Another American, Jim Drake, came to the conclusion that the most effective form of freesailing system could be provided by connecting the base of the mast to the board by a universal joint. This allowed complete freedom for the mast to be pivoted in all directions. Drake was fortunate enough to have a friend, Hoyle Schweitzer, who helped him overcome many of the technical hitches involved in the design. A United States Patent application, was soon made for the appropriately named 'windsurfer'. Drake and Schweitzer then risked a small production run, initially supplying their friends. The windsurfer did not sell up to its expectations, so Schweitzer bought Drake out of his half of the patent for what, with hindsight, appears to have been a nominal fee.

To this day, the windsurfer is still being manufactured in its original 'flat board' format, although the components have been greatly modified. Gone are the wooden fin, the teak boom and the antique mastfoot of yesteryear. That the basic windsurfer design has survived more or less intact is due to its immense stability: it is still an ideal beginner's board, or an excellent longboard freestyle unit. Windsurfer is also a recognised one design class for racing.

With true Californian entrepreneurial spirit, Schweitzer tried to protect his investment by registering the patent in as many countries as possible. Sales suddenly took a sharp upward turn, and the new Californian toy caught the imagination of the Europeans. A Dutch company, Ten Cate, began importing into Europe, and the windsurfer soon took off in Holland, Germany and France. By 1973, the parent company could not keep up with demand, so Ten Cate began to manufacture in Europe under licence. Within only a couple of years many other European plastic manufacturers realized the potential and set up rival – albeit unlicensed – production. Lengthy court wrangles ensued, and most manufacturers eventually resigned themselves to paying Schweitzer's 7½% patent fee.

Competitive windsurfing grew at the same hectic pace as the commercial developments. The Californians were soon into freestyle and tricks, an aspect of the sport which is now less prominent. The original windsurfer was the perfect machine for all sorts of spins and tacks. The pinnacle of freestyle performance was the rail ride, which took – and takes – a fair amount of acrobatic skill to execute. In Europe, competition went another way in the form of a more traditional type of triangular course racing, based on yacht racing. It became apparent that the windsurfer had its drawbacks on the long upwind legs. Boards that worked more on the principle of a yacht proved better suited to triangle racing. These – mostly European – boards were designed with high volume and rounded hulls. They worked so much better in light airs that it became necessary to divide the fleet into two categories. The old flat boards were now classed as Division 1, a category for the recreational sailor, while Division II, with its rounded displacement boards, was tailored more for the serious racer.

In late 1977 two Hawaiian sailors, Horgan and Stanley, found an elegant solution to the problem of controlling the board in heavy surf and high winds. Heading out through heavy waves, the rider would often get airborne, and separated from the board in the process. The solution to the problem was footstraps, an invention that radically changed the face of windsurfing and introduced the now familiar funboard. With the advantage of footstraps, and with improved board design, control became easier, and more challenging conditions could be attempted. Throughout the first hand-shaped custom boards were tailored to the individual rider's needs. Daggerboards were now dispensed with, especially above force four; boards were steered by a combination of rig and foot pressure through the straps. Footsteering facility led to a new high-speed turn, the carve gybe. Heading out, the sailors could

The original windsurfer.

hop off the waves and maintain a modicum of control. Stories and pictures of the Hawaiian wave jumpers soon spread to Europe and funboard mass-production hit the European market.

Sail and rig technology developed along-side the new board shapes at a similar rate of knots. The old favourite triangular rags were modified to suit the surf, the boom was

Old style sail.

Modern sail with foot batten.

shortened and the clew, or back end of the sail, was raised to avoid the breaking waves.

In the consistent Hawaiian winds sailors soon evolved the waterstart. Instead of tiring and tricky uphauling in the surf, the pioneers found the strong tradewinds were sufficient to pull them directly onto the board. The new higher aspect sails were almost a pre-requisite for such fancy new moves. Almost overnight, a great deal of windsurfing hardware became obsolete. Demand for the latest high-tech kit was massive. The sport and its associated industry multiplied apace.

'Radical' is the only word to describe subsequent developments. Early stars such as Mike Waltze and Robby Naish now found they could use boards which were in fact too small to uphaul in a conventional fashion. The waterstart-only boards, or 'sinkers' as they became known, were not only smaller, but as a consequence lighter and more manoeuver-able, both on the water and in the air. In fact, they were more like wind-surfboards; many sailors took to cutting down large surfboards to the dimensions of the new style waveboards. After a visit to Maui, Jurgen Honscheid returned to Europe with one of these converted surfboards. At the Weymouth speed trials he delighted the crowd by his turn of speed and sweeping carved gybes. As one can imagine, it was not long before the more traditional Division I and II Boards were pushed aside by the new generation of funboards. Funboard racing along adapted courses became the new craze, with shortened upwind legs for triangle racing and all-downwind slalom runs – all gybes and no tacks.

1984 was a watershed year in windsurfing; for the first time it figured as an Olympic sport. The surf-bum, it appeared, was now poised to enter the yachting scene. In the first competition the flying Dutchman, Van den Berg, took the honours over a typical yachting course using a one-design board which was was considered out of date even at the time.

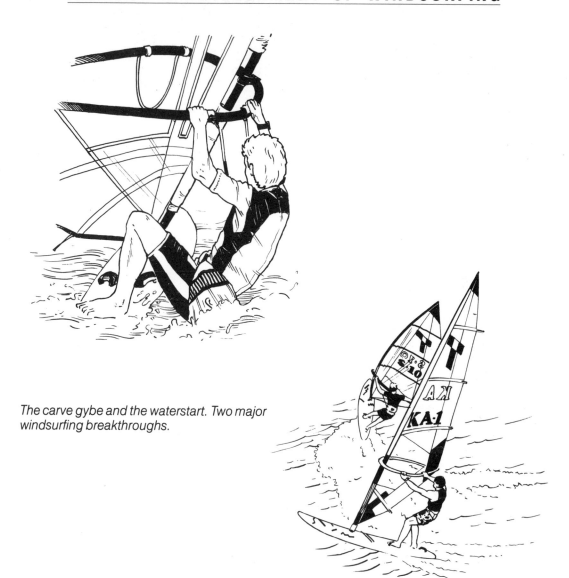

The carve gybe and the waterstart. Two major windsurfing breakthroughs.

Hawaii strengthened its position as the research and development capital of the world with the introduction of fully battened sails, a concept borrowed from the world of yachting – the catamaran sail in particular. Now boom lengths could be reduced even further, giving more scope for riding higher surf and sailing stronger winds. With the benefit of the first really user-friendly rigs the top sailors perfected manoeuvres such as the barrel roll or backwind loop – these quickly became the new buzzwords among the radical sailing fraternity. Using these Hawaiian innovations to full advantage, Maui-based Fred Haywood, using extra battens below the boom and a wing-foiled mast,

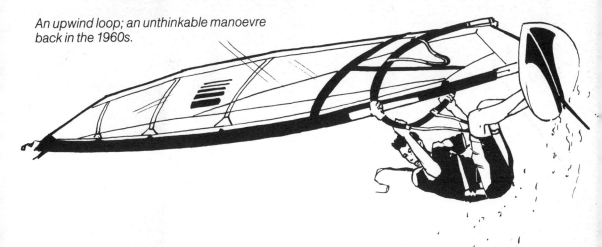

An upwind loop; an unthinkable manoevre back in the 1960s.

shattered the 30-knot barrier at Weymouth speed week in 1986. This is still regarded as one of the sport's great milestones – the four-minute mile of windsurfing. The foot batten played an important part in this achievement, offering as it did a major improvement in rig-stability. It was realized that sails would work with either long or short battens above the boom, provided that there was a full-length batten below it.

It could be said that at this point the sport of windsurfing had reached maturity. No longer was it necessary to discard equipment every few months in the knowledge that technology had made vast strides in the intervening period. There might be marginal improvements, offering marginally improved performance, but no major innovations.

The latest radical development occurred in the winter months of 1987. A loop downwind as opposed to the previous upwind rotation was successfully attempted, once again in Hawaii. Every proficient short board sailor

tried to emulate the new forward roll, some successfully and some not – never have so many broken noses been sustained in the name of sport in the course of one short season! This rolling motion has latterly evolved into more of a cartwheeling rotation, and is without question one of the most spectacular windsurfing manoeuvres to be seen.

The turn of the decade saw Robby Naish, hitherto the undisputed king of the world funboard cup, knocked off his throne by Bjorn Dunkerbeck. Naish had led the way since sport's inception with a long succession of World Cup titles.

Windsurfing now seems to be settling down into a steadier pattern of growth. The majority of new boards are now funboards of some description. The longer board of 370 cm or thereabouts are ideal for novices, while shorter, hybrid models are more suited to intermediate or experienced sailors. Never has there been a better time to take up the challenge. Good equipment, recognized schools, books and videos all help to minimize the pains of learning, and bring the pleasures of this exciting sport within the reach of everyone.

Peter Hart, RYA Trainer and top flight competitor.

EQUIPMENT & TERMINOLOGY

A casual observer, glancing along the beach on a breezy summer's day, will be struck by the variety of boards on display. Makes and models obviously differ, but there are also differences in size, shape and, of course, in colour and artwork. Quality of boards can vary immensely. The prospective purchaser would be wise not to economize too much on equipment, but, before buying, make up your mind exactly what you are looking for; there is no point in buying a Ferrari when a Ford will do the job quite adequately.

The materials used and method of construction have an important bearing on the prices. By far the cheapest construction method is polyethylene moulding. Polyethylene is a type of plastic that lends itself well to mass production around a foam core. Boards of this material are very robust and will withstand a lot of stress both on and off the water. If they are damaged, which is very rare, they are, however, difficult to repair at home. The surface finish is not always perfect, but this is not of critical importance on a purely family or recreational board.

ABS- or ASA-type harder plastics tend to give a better quality moulding, but this must be weighed against increased cost. Most boards of this construction are made in two halves and are joined by a thin seam along the edge or rail. Hull finish is important for water flow characteristics and overall performance. ASA boards are also much stiffer than their polyethylene counterparts. ASA is a little more susceptible to damage, but easier to repair. The better quality mass-produced boards tend to be of this material.

The best moulded boards are made of fibreglass materials. Fibreglass is very strong, weight for weight even stronger than steel. There are basically two resins used in conjunction with the fibreglass, polyester and epoxy, the latter being used only by top performers, as the extra strength it offers (especially in combination with Kevlar and carbon fibreglass) does not come cheap.

True performance freaks often prefer a board which is custom-made to their own specification. Instead of using a mould, the custom board producer will have the foam core tailored by hand by a shaper and then enveloped in fibreglass. This handbuilt approach is extremely time-consuming, and expensive. The majority of custom-made boards tend to be for specialist wave use, competitive speed trials or slalom racing. In terms of performance they are second to none.

At the end of the day, the performance of the board is only as good as the design and manufacturing skill put into it. Among the design parameters involved are length, width, volume, plan shape, rocker line, rail shape and underwater profile. Basically, the longer and wider the board is, the more stable it is, say for a beginner. The shorter it gets the more proficient the sailor will need to be. Volume determines the board's flotation and it is measured in litres. The higher the volume, the easier it is to sail. Beginners' boards are often about 250 litres, while an out-and-out wave board may be down to as little as 75 litres. The heavier the sailor, the more volume is required to keep him afloat.

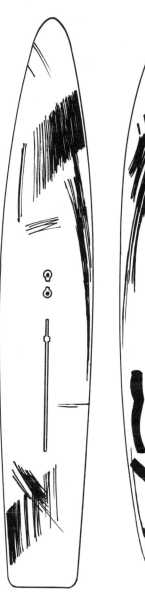

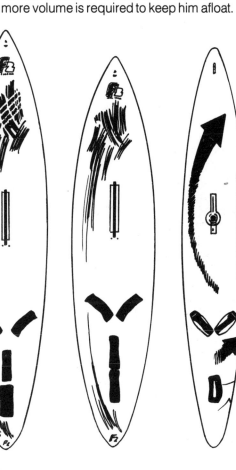

Lechner or div II	*Flatboard or div I*	*Slalomboard*	*Waveboard*	*Speedboard*
380 × 68 cm	*370 × 66 cm*	*275 × 58 cm*	*260 × 56 cm*	*265 × 45 cm*

The plan shape and in particular the position of the wildest point will affect the board's manoeuvrability. The further forward the maximum width, the more directionally stable the board will be; the further aft, the greater the manoeuvrability. The curve or rocker line of the hull will also affect manoeuvrability and speed. A board with a shallow rocker, such as a racing board, will have great speed but may not navigate corners as well as a board with a more banana-like, wave-board type of rocker line. A low rocker line is quicker to plane. The rail shape will determine how the board grips the water. A full rail, usually with sharp edges, is quick to plane and good upwind, though it can be difficult to gybe as it can bounce out easily and lose grip. A soft rail has better gripping qualities, but is not as fast or as quick to plane.

As for underwater profiles, most modern hulls incorporate a certain amount of vee which facilitates directional stability and rail-to-rail steering. As well as this, many funboards incorporate concaves or other channelled effects, all in the name of earlier pick up onto the plane.

Plainly, board design is not as simple as it appears! A change of as little as 1 cm in any of the above variables can radically alter a board's behaviour. But the principles for specific uses are more or less constant. For example, a course-racing board will always require a low rocker line, full and sharp rails, good volume about the mast and some vee in the tail. Beginner boards are long and wide, flat-hulled (for stability) and high in volume. All these features make life much easier for the learner. The true triangle racer's machine is similar to the flatboard in that it is long and high in volume, as much as 300 litres. It is not suitable for the novices as it has a rounded instead of a flat hull, which makes it unstable. It does, however, perform well to windward in light airs, working on a similar displacement principles as a yacht. These Division II boards are popular for lightwind inland sailing.

The funboard has latterly superseded the Division I and II boards. The funboard has retracting daggers and footstraps, allowing it to be steered by foot pressure once planing. The larger funboards are flatboard hybrids and can be used to learn on by anyone with a reasonable sense of balance. A funboard for learners will also take the sailor well into the intermediate stages of sailing. It is obvious why the vast majority of new boards sold today are versatile funboards between 350–370 cm in length.

Funboards are available in many sizes, down from the beginner's model through the intermediate size of around 330 cm, to the advanced 295 cm size and finally onto the expert's 265 cm. As a general rule the smaller the board the more wind it needs to get it going. Often sailors will have two boards, one for lighter and the other for stronger airs.

Sails

The theory of forward motion by wind and sail power is quite simple. As the wind flows towards the sail it separates about the mast and travels along each side of the sail. Due to the curvature of the sail, the wind affects each side differently; on the leeward side the air is accelerated, resulting in a pressure reduction. On the windward, or nearer, side the air slows down causing a high pressure zone. This action of high pressure pushing towards the low pressure area creates the drive that propels the craft forwards.

The natural direction of this force will push the board sideways and forwards. It is the function of the daggerboard and/or fin to resist this sideways push and ensure that there is forward motion with minimal lateral drift.

Commonly, new boards are equipped with a sail between 5.5 and 6 square metres, which is ideal for use in lighter airs. However, as the wind increases it become physically very difficult to hold such a big sail. It is then

Points of sailing.

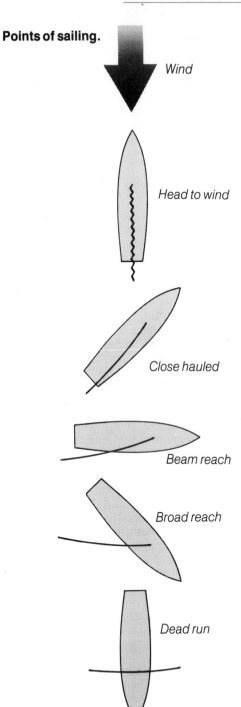

Wind

Head to wind

Close hauled

Beam reach

Broad reach

Dead run

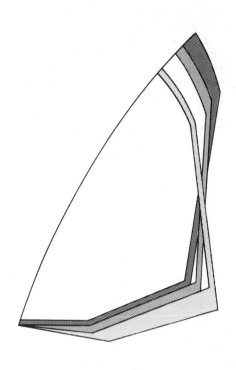

Aspect ratio High Medium Low

time to change down to a smaller, more manageable size. Depending on make and model a manufacturer can offer sails ranging from a 3-square metre handkerchief up to 9 square metres. The extreme sizes are for specialist use only, the 'handkerchiefs' for high-wind wavesailors and the mega sails for light wind racing. For recreational sailing the novice should choose a realistic size, depending on his body weight and height. Children are a special case. Although a child will be able to use the same hull as an adult, he or she will generally require a special rig. This not only incorporates a small sail, but also a light, short mast and a narrow tubed boom, which is much easier to uphaul out of the water.

WINDSURFING

The windsurfing sail consists of a series of shaped panels which are taped and sewn together. The cloth is generally of Dacron or Mylar material. Dacron is cheaper and is also more hard-wearing. After extended use, Dacron woven texture can stretch, leaving the sail tired or blown out, and handling characteristics are seriously affected. Mylar is a more stable material, retaining its original shape for a longer time. It tends to be used for more high-performance sails but involves considerable extra cost. Mylar is more fragile than Dacron. Some cloth manufacturers incorporate a scrim into the Mylar in an attempt to increase its anti-tear qualities. At the top end of performance sails, a monofilm membrane substance is used to replace the sailcloth. These totally clear sails are extremely light and have excellent air-flow characteristics. However, a small hole or puncture in the membrane can result in the total destruction of the sail.

Sails can be divided into two categories: soft sails, which have an unsupported luff area, and hard sails which have full-length battens supporting the whole sail.

Soft sails were the first to be developed, and are generally lighter in weight. With its short leech battens a soft sail is ideal for the beginner. It is easier to uphaul as it does not cradle water like the hard sail. When hauled up the front panel will flutter in the breeze, allowing the learner to get a feel for the wind and its direction; some hybrid soft sails are preferred by recreational short-board sailors and waveriders who prefer the luffing method of depowering the sail.

The most popular of all sails today is the hard-set RAF or rotating asymmetric foil. The idea is that the battens rotate about the mast, allowing the sail to set on the leeward side, a point where it is efficient and stable. The

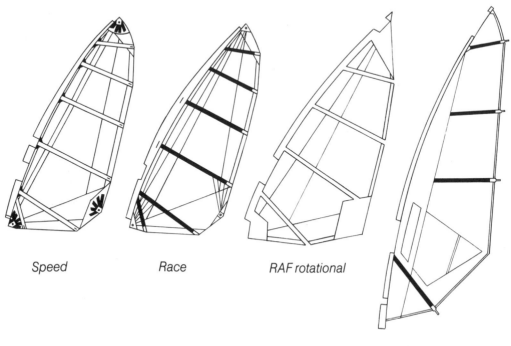

Speed   *Race*   *RAF rotational*

Soft sail

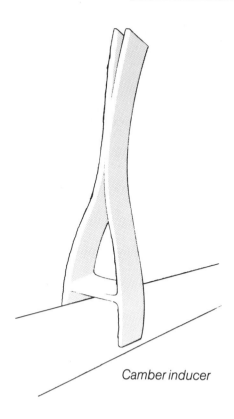

Camber inducer

Masts

Masts made in Europe, the home base of all the major board manufacturers, are standard in diameter, and therefore completely inter-changeable. These 48.5 mm spars are by far the most common worldwide. In the US, a 46 mm mast is still produced as masts are usually made from fibreglass which is both strong and flexible. Such masts are ideal for any recreational use. Specialist racers demand superior performance, so they look to aluminium for a stiffer and more lightweight alternative. If money is no object, carbon-fibre hybrids offers the ultimate in lightness. Generally, the sailor should try and fit the sail to the appropriate mast. Racing sails, with less luff bend, will only set on a mast which is very stiff, while most recreational sails will set adequately on anything. Usually, a sail manufacturer will recommend a particular mast for a sail as its luff curve will be made to match up with a specific model. Two-part masts are widely acceptable today. They are much easier to store than full-length masts – whether it be at home or in the cargo hold of a plane – and are increasingly popular.

ultimate hard sail is an extension of the RAF idea known as the camber inducer. This component is like a plastic tuning fork which rotates around the mast while also sup-porting the leading edge of the sail very firmly. Camber-induced sails are by far the most powerful, efficient and stable sails, making them a must for funboard and speed sailors. An induced sail would, however, be of no use to a novice, and should be avoided at all costs.

Increasingly, variable-mode sails are finding favour. These all-rounders offer compromise where inducers and battens can be introduced or removed to suit prevailing conditions. They certainly seem to work, but are not well regarded by purists, who are inclined to advance that old argument about the Jack of all trades who is master of none!

Booms

The boom, or wishbone, is elliptical in shape and consists of two aluminium tubes which are coated with a soft rubber grip. These two curved tubes are joined together at each end by moulded plastic fittings.

The front end fitting is critical; a good front end will give a solid mast-to-boom connection, making steering much more positive. For years, booms were connected using assorted forms of lashings. It was quite an achievement to get the connection as tight as it should be. Nowadays, more and more manufacturers are reverting to clamp-on front ends. These eccentric-looking devices assure a fast, firm fit which is almost foolproof, and a great boon to both beginner and expert.

The rear boom end should incorporate some form of cleat and pulley system. It is much easier to set the sail using the boom's integral pulley system. Be sure, however, not to rely exclusively on the cleats. Always secure the end of the line with a couple of half hitches.

Most booms are adjustable in body length, so that one boom can be used to accommodate a range of sail sizes. The adjustment is achieved either by telescopic or by add-on sections. Telescopic booms usually adjust by about 50 cm up from their base length. The adjustment is governed either by holes in the main tube or by rear end fitting. Most booms adjust in 5 cm increments, which makes it easy to get the clew of the sail to the desired position near the rear boom end. Telescopic booms do need a little attention to maintain their slide-trombone action. They must be kept dirt- and sand-free by frequent flushing out with fresh water.

Add-on booms are less common, and usually restricted to the upper echelons of the sport, where sailors insist on the greatest possible strength and lightness from their equipment.

A boom's inherent strength depends mainly on the quality of the aluminium tubing. The chances of breakage are increased if the adjustable boom spends most of its life at its maximum extension.

Telescopic, and with add-on extensions

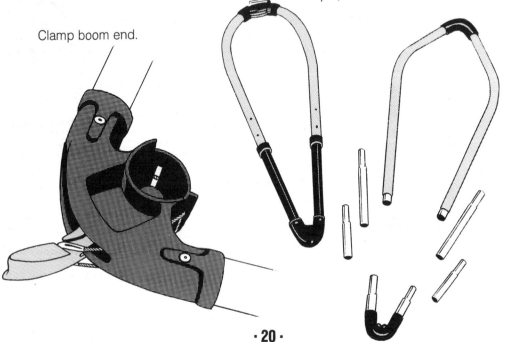

Clamp boom end.

The J&B tandem is one of the more unusual speed machines, captured here at Sotavento, Fuerteventura.

Kids rigs

Children often find the chore of uphauling just too much for them. This problem is seldom overcome by simply using an adult's high-wind sail, no matter how small it may be. Ideally, the youngster requires a rig devised specially for him. Sails on such rigs are small in area, between 2 and 3 sq m. The sail must be used with a short, lightweight mast, which greatly aids easy uphauling. The boom fits into a luff cut out which is large, leaving plenty of room to raise the boom as the child gets bigger.

Good quality kids' rigs also incorporate small-diameter boom tubes, which are much easier for small hands than the standard diameter. As long as the rig is adapted for use by a child, there is no problem about using it in conjunction with the hull that is suitable for an adult beginner.

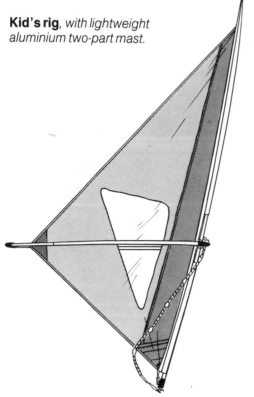

Kid's rig, *with lightweight aluminium two-part mast.*

Footstraps.

Footstraps

The advantages of footstraps only become apparent in planing conditions, when the straps not only help in steering but also keep the sailor in contact with the board when the going gets rough. Virtually all modern boards are designed to accommodate footstraps. It must be said, though, that unless the sailor is reasonably competent, the footstraps may just get in the way. The learner may also be tempted to use them for a feeling of security when there is insufficient wind. In such a case it is better to remove the straps until competence improves.

If the board has a number of possible footstrap positions, not unusual on large funboards, the front set of training straps are best for the beginner, because they are easiest to get into. As the sailor becomes more proficient, he may add other straps or move the existing ones aft.

Most footstraps are adjustable in size, usually by means of velcro tongues situated beneath the soft exterior cover. For both safety and comfort the strap must be correctly adjusted; if it is too loose, this may result in a twisted ankle or worse mishap. The strap should just fit comfortably over the bridge of the foot.

Daggerboards

The daggerboard, which fits in a slot just behind the mast, is found on all longer boards. It is an indispensable aid for upwind work, especially in light airs.

In the old days, the sailor had to bend down and withdraw the daggerboard completely for the off the wind points of sailing. Modern daggerboards pivot fore and aft, while the majority will retract fully up into the hull when necessary, for example on downwind reaches.

Daggerboards vary in size, the larger variety being found in Division I and II where upwind ability is most important. Funboards designed for slightly higher winds have much shorter and narrower daggerboards; these are perfectly adequate, since it is easier to point upwind in stronger airs. Once funboards shrink below 320 cm, daggerboards become redundant, since fin pressure alone will drive the hull upwind.

Recreational longboards tend to be supplied with plastic daggerboards. Racing sailors prefer the stiffer and therefore more stable effect of a wooden or aluminium daggerboard, often retracting behind a watertight flushing strip on the hull.

Mast tracks

All good new production boards have some form of mast-track system. The track is useful as it gives scope to position the mast fore or aft, depending on the wind or the point of sailing.

In light airs the board will plane earlier if the mast is positioned forwards; this will also feel more comfortable when big sails with longer boom lengths are used. As the wind picks up, the board will perform better with the mast place further aft. If at all in doubt, leave the mast positioned centrally in its track. A forward mast position is better for going upwind as the board's effective waterline length is increased.

For any form of triangular racing you must be able to move the mast position while in motion, so as to get maximum performance on all points of sailing. Many race-tuned boards and funboards have a sliding track which can be operated by a foot pedal during the race. Shorter boards and in particular custom boards tend to have fin-box type deck fittings into which the mast foot is fixed. These are very strong and are capable of withstanding the punishment a board has to endure in high winds.

The mast base, including the rubber universal joint, can be attached to the track in a variety of ways, depending on the make and model of the particular board. The mast base will often include an adjustable extension which can be raised or lowered depending on the luff length of the sail in use.

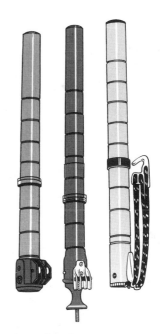

Mast tracks *extensions.*

Fins

The fin is the component which gives the windsurfer its directional stability. Without the fin the board will just not steer.

There are now so many varieties of fin on the market, differing in shape, size and colour, that it is little wonder that the beginner gets confused. The crucial consideration is that the fin should suit the board. The larger the board, the larger the fin needs to be. Deep fins are particularly useful for going upwind, and are thus important for longboards and longboard racing. These larger fins work well in light winds as they can counteract the force of the big sail often used in such airs. As winds pick up, board speeds increase, and naturally the resistance encountered by the fin is increased. A small fin is therefore better suited to stronger airs.

The more upright a fin is in shape, the more stability it offers. On the other hand, the more swept or raked back it is, the more man-oeuvrability it offers, at the expense of speed. The large, upright fin is used for upwind racing, and the swept-back fin, usually small, is used for wavesailing.

Foil shape also affects a fin's performance. Like the sail, the fuller it is, the better the acceleration, the flatter the profile, the faster it is. A clean foil shape is always a good sign; water travels more smoothly over a clean foil, which also offers better grip.

The stiffness of the fin should be given some consideration. A stiff fin that fits well in its box will offer much better performance than a pliable one. Much of the stiffness is dictated by the material from which the fin is made. Plastic fins, although cheaper, tend to be very flexible, and lead directly to spin out. Spin out, or cavitation, occurs when planing; bubbles travel down the fin causing it to lose its grip in the water and directional stability is suddenly lost. Stiffer fins, either moulded or custom-made from fibreglass, are less susceptible to spin out, but inevitably, they cost a good deal more.

Many ingenious attempts have been made to counter spin out, the most successful being to alter the shape of the fin (the so-called football fin) and to add fences across the fin. The current favourite is a small nick at the base of the fin, called a cutaway fin, and a vertical slot in the fin, a window fin. Both these designs are widely used, even though they detract a little from the fin's potential top speed and acceleration.

Fins.

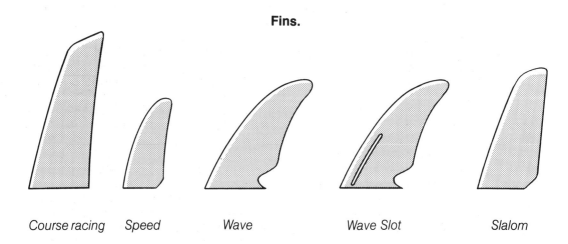

Course racing   Speed   Wave   Wave Slot   Slalom

Wetsuits.

Wetsuits

Windsurfing without some form of wet suit is not recommended. Apart from the discomfort of getting cold, there is an element of danger that should not be ignored. The effect of cold water and wind is to reduce the body's core temperature. In extreme cases the chill factor develops into hypothermia, when the sailor can easily slide into unconsciousness and die.

All wet suits are made out of a jigsaw of shaped neoprene rubber panels. These panels are lined on one or both sides with nylon. The single lined material presents a bare rubber surface to the water, which drips straight off, and is therefore less prone to cause wind chill. The double lined materials are slightly less slippery, but have harder wearing characteristics.

The method used to join the rubber panels together affects the wet suit's thermal qualities. The more traditional joint is a mauser tape and stitch used most commonly on long john and bolero type suits. This seam is not well sealed and therefore a lot of water can pass in and out of the suit via the seams. A suit of this type is alright for general use, but not suitable for really cold conditions. By far the simplest join is the overlock stitch, popular with all the mass producers of wet suits. Like the mauser, it is best suited to warm weather garments, as it allows seepage through the seam. The last and by far the warmest seam is the blind stitch. All seams are glued and then stitched, making it almost watertight. All good winder 'steamers' are blindstitched. This is a labour-intensive process, and therefore expensive.

Warm weather suits tend to be made of rubber 2 or 3 mm thick. The thinness of the material makes these suits easy to overlock, and their flexibility makes them very comfortable to wear. The real ice-breaker sailors require 5-mm body suits that are blindstitched. In practice, most suits are of variable thicknesses; winter suits often have 5-mm body panels, but with 3-mm panels in areas which are flexed a lot, such as the arms and the backs of the knees.

To work effectively, a wetsuit needs to be a snug fit. A well-fitting suit will trap a thin layer of the water that gets into the suit. This thin layer is then warmed up by body heat. Clearly, a loose fitting suit that takes in too much water is not going to have good thermal properties; every time you take a dip you will get cooled down. Always try a wet suit on before buying it. Remember that what you need is a well-fitting suit, not a fancy coloured one!

The style of the suit may vary from a simple neoprene vest up to an all in one full steamer. Generally it is better to err on the side of being too warm than too cold. Where there are wide seasonal variations in temperature, it makes sense to have a wardrobe of suits to suit the season.

Harnesses.

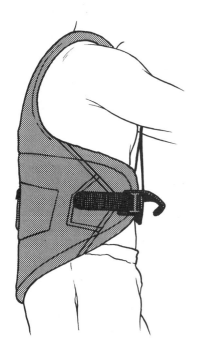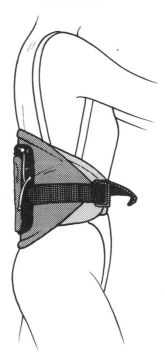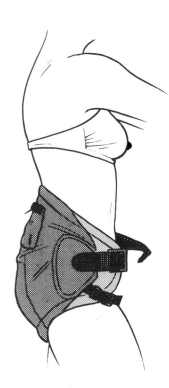

| *Chest* | *Waist* | *Seat* |

Harnesses

Modern windsurfing harnesses do not provide much in the way of buoyancy, and should not be regarded as buoyancy aids. The main function of the harness is to ease the strain on the arms and back, it is an energy-saving device. The large hook at the front of the harness clips over a line attached to the boom at approximately waist level. When hooked in, the harness then transfers the pull of the rig through the whole of the sailor's body, so that the strain on the arms is greatly reduced. Without a harness it would be impossible to sail for long without being exhausted. Correct use of the harness also makes for better control, and allows the use of bigger sails than would otherwise be possible. Funboards sail better with harnessed riders, especially when the wind picks up. The skills of early plane and better manoeuvreing are enhanced by use of the harness, since it is easier to distribute boom weight through the mast foot via the boom. The harness is not much use to the absolute beginner, or to anyone sailing in very light airs. The novice would be well advised to get the hang of windsurfing before getting into the habit of wearing this item of equipment.

There are three styles of harness available: chest, seat and waist. The seat harness is by far the most popular, suitable for recreational sailing and racing. The seat's lower hook position gives it maximum leverage on the rig, making it a must for any racer, either slalom or speed. The waist harness is also geared to recreational use, primarily on shortboards. This harness offers great freedom of movement for the upper and lower body, and consequently finds favour with wavesailors.

The chest harness is a survival from the past, being the original form of windsurfing harness. It offers the best buoyancy of all harnesses, but still not enough to float an unconscious sailor. Some wavesailors like the small amount of protection offered by this harness.

Roof-rack systems

Virtually all windsurfers, unless they live right on the beach, need some sort of transport. For most sailors, therefore, a roof rack is an indispensable item of equipment.

Roof racks, like cars, come in various shapes and sizes, but usually a traditional Thule or Terzo rack will fit any car with a gutter. These sturdier racks are by no means cheap, but they do the job best, especially if more than one board needs to be transported. Cars without gutters may be fitted with the appropriate gutterless rack, generally made by the manufacturer of the car.

As a rule of thumb the racks should be positioned as far apart as possible, so as to spread the load. Nose forwards and fin upwards is the normal configuration. If two boards are carried it's best to stack one on top of the other, rather than side by side. Be sure to strap the board down securely, using a proper webbing strap with a buckle. Elasticated rope and bits of string will not do, nor for that matter will badly worn straps. To secure hundreds of pounds worth of gear with tatty bits of twine may prove to be an expensive and very dangerous error.

Board insurance

Board insurance makes sense; it is available in most countries, and premiums are usually not too excessive. Insuring a board is like insuring a car; third-party liability is essential, safeguarding you should you run into another sailor and inflict injury on him or her and damage his or her equipment. Comprehensive cover is well worth the additional cost, and you may well be pleased you took it if the board is stolen from the roof of your car. A mechanism to lock board and rig securely to the roof of the car is advisable. Not only does this act as a deterrent, it may be a prerequisite for insurance.

The Board and Rig

1 Nose or bow. Sometimes fitted with a rubber bumper and towing eye.

2 Tail or stern.

3 Skeg or fin. Used singularly, or in triangular formations.

4 Daggerboard. Sometimes made to retract into the hull.

5 Footstraps. Fitted in several configurations.

6 Mastfoot well. Often allowing two mast track positions. An alternative is a sliding mast track.

7 Daggerboard well. Reinforced and built into the hull.

8 Mast or spar. Made from fibreglass or aluminium.

9 Mastfoot and universal joint. Made to lock into track, or release under tension.

10 Boom or wishbone. Fixed or variable length.

11 Sail clew. Reinforced with metal eyelet.

12 Outhaul. Sometimes used with a pulley system and tied off with a cleat on the boom.

13 Boom front end. Often with grip handle.

14 Inhaul. Tied off with a cleat.

15 Uphaul. Knotted to give grip. Hawaiian type is soft with elasticated core.

16 Shock-cord. For use with regular uphaul

17 Downhaul. Sometimes used with a pulley system, and tied off with a cleat on the mastfoot.

18 Safety cord. Joins the mastfoot to the board.

19 Battens. Fitted into batten pockets.

20 Leech of the sail.

21 Foot of the sail.

22 Luff of the sail.

23 Mast sleeve.

24 Head of the sail.

25 Mast head.

26 Tack of the sail.

27 Roach.

28 Footroach.

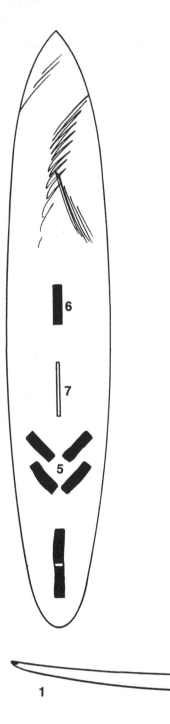

Plan view. (below) The positioning of the footstraps, mast wells, and daggerboard case, is a primary consideration in board manufacture.

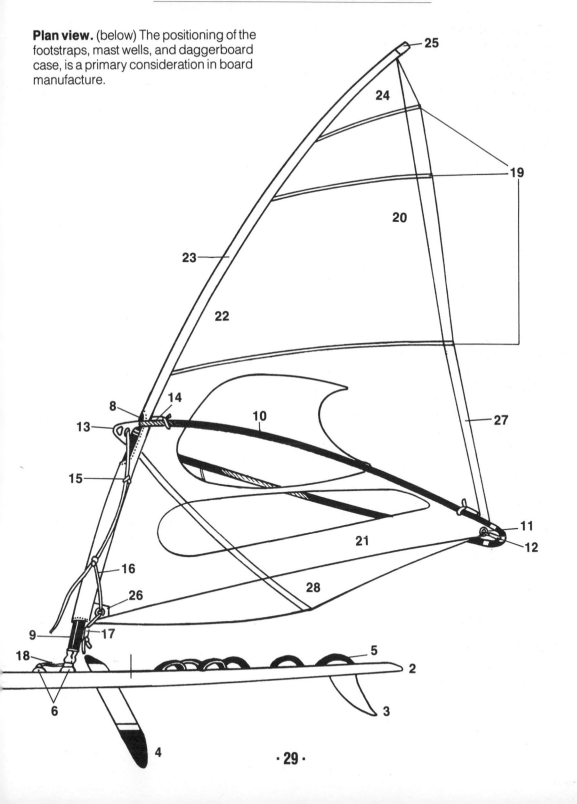

WINDSURFING TERMINOLOGY

Apparent wind   A combination of the true wind and the wind created upon the sail by the board's forward motion.

Battens   These long thin strips made of fibreglass are bone-type structures which add additional support to the sail. They are extensively used to support areas of excessive roach which would otherwise be limp.

Bear away   A steering manoeuvre that takes the nose of the board away from the wind.

Beam reach   Or close reach, is a course directly across or at 90° to the wind. This relatively fast point of sailing is also the easiest to adopt in the early stages.

Broad reach   Another reach that is further off the wind than a beam reach. Typically, 110–130° off the wind. It is by far the fastest point of sailing. As such, it is usually adopted by high wind speed and slalom sailors in pursuit of mach 1.

Camber inducer   A tuning-fork type mechanism which fits to the leading edge of the sail. In conjunction with battens, the inducer stabilizes the front edge and luff area of the sail to make it more aerodynamically efficient.

Cavitation   Sometimes called spin-out, an action that occurs when the fins are aerated and lose their grip in the water. In practice the back end of the board moves radically away from its track and all directional stability is lost. A proficient sailor can recover from cavitation by slowing down and sheeting out to regain grip.

Clew   Region of the sail that is adjacent to the rear end of the boom. This reinforced area incorporates an eyelet for the outhaul rope to pass through.

Close haul   Sometimes called a beat, where the board is projected as closely into the wind as possible. Following this approximately 45° course towards the wind is usually done in an attempt to reach a goal upwind, via a series of tacks.

Edge of the sail   In conjunction with battens, the inducer stabilizes the front edge and luff area of the sail to make it more aerodynamically efficient.

Eye of the wind   The direction from which the true wind is coming.

Harness   This distributes the pull of the sail away from the sailor's arms towards his or her body. The waist, chest or seat harness aids longer and more efficient sailing.

Head   The top area of the sail close to the tip of the mast.

Head to wind   A point where the nose of the board points directly into the eye of the wind. The board will have no motion and the sail will flap freely in the breeze along the centreline of the board.

Head up   The opposite of bearing away: the nose of the board moves towards the wind.

Hull   The windsurfing board with the rig removed.

Leech   The back, or trailing edge of the sail.

Planing   A trimming situation, when the board is skimming along with the least resistance from the water. Usually associated with winds in excess of a force 3.

Rig   The combination of mast, sail, boom and mastfoot.

Roach   The area of the sail which lies outside an imaginery line connecting the head to the clew (leech roach) and the clew to the tack (foot roach).

Run   The furthest point of sailing off the wind (a complete 180°). The nose of the board points directly downwind, opposite the head-to-wind position.

Sinker   A board that will not support the dead weight of the sailor and rig when not in motion. As the term suggests, it sinks below the surface. The volume, or flotation in the board is measured in litres. One litre will be displaced by a one kilogram load: an 85-litre board, for example, should float a 75-kilo sailor, plus rig.

Tack   The area of the sail nearest to the mastfoot, reinforced and with eyelet for the downhaul. Also, a zig-zagging of the board on a close haul, to make ground upwind.

Universal joint   The part of the windsurfer that allows a 'freesail' system, the invention upon which the whole concept of the sport is based. The joint connects the rig to the board, its mechanical or rubber structure allows the mast to be tilted in any plane about 360°.

Wipe out   That all-too-common early bath from only too regular pilot error!

THE SPORT –
A GUIDE

In the early stages, competitive windsurfing was modelled on dinghy sailing, and similar rules applied, derived from the International Yacht Racing Union. With the development of funboarding, it soon became apparent that new rules would be needed. The constraints of the I.Y.R.U. rules became evident as funboarding developed into flattened triangle racing, slalom, and wave sailing. These three separate developments now form three disciplines in the World Tour, in which top professionals compete. On a national level, most countries now have their own circuits, which form the training grounds for aspiring international sailors.

Speedsailing events demand special conditions of wind and water, which means at the highest level at least, a few out-of-the-way locations. Speedsters are a race apart, and do not often get competitively involved in other areas of the sport.

The artistic element of windsurfing is something that should not be overlooked; it cannot be denied that it offers a very stylish mode of self expression to the expert performer. This, no doubt, is what motivates the novices floundering in the shallows as much as the expert executing perfect gybes and jumps on the waves off Maui.

Racing

As the sport has evolved over the years, so the rules governing racing have changed. Happily, these changes have been gradually simplified.

The traditional categories of Division II roundboards, Division I flatboards and Division 0 funboards have now given way to two classes. Lechner class is the Olympic class, and replaces Division II. This change to a one-design has had the effect of giving the fading Division II circuits a new lease of life, with the added attraction that a round board sailor can now aim for Olympic honours.

To ensure uniformity, the Lechner comes with its own rig. The sail, designed with light airs in mind, is 7.5 m^2 in area. Rather than change sails, the Lechner sailor will more often insert a mast of different stiffness: this helps to keep costs down. It's worth noting, too, that Lechner boards retain their value well. The previous Division II boards were always being rendered obsolete, which was bad news for resale values.

Although the course is totally at the discretion of the officer of the day, the usual Olympic-type course is the 'P' course. This involves all points of sailing, starting on a beat (traditionally the leg where most ground is

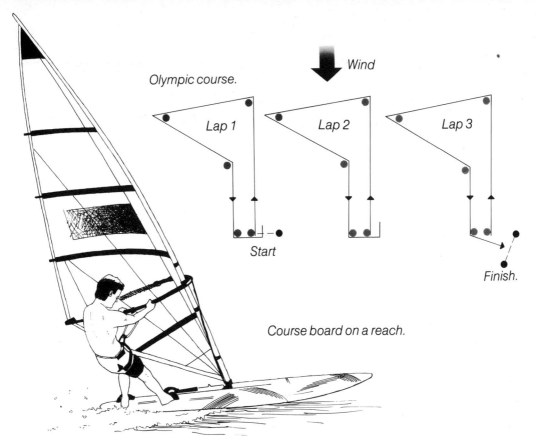

Olympic course.

Wind

Lap 1

Lap 2

Lap 3

Start

Finish.

Course board on a reach.

won or lost) onto a close reach, a broad reach and a run.

By far the largest fleet is the funboard class. This evolved as most of the hybrid long funboards, originally Division O, fell into the Division I specifications. These funboards, after all, were just refined flatboards. Funboard class has no real rig restrictions or design parameters. Often a maximum sail area of $7.5\,m^2$ is imposed, or on an amateur level a restriction to 3 rigs. Amateur levels, particularly in Europe, tend to restrict the competitors to production equipment only. Not only is this good news for the mass producers, it is also fairer for the racers, as they stand a better chance of eventual sponsorship and in the meantime don't have to invest in expensive custom boards. The top racers can proceed to the production world cup competition.

The top event for the funboard class is the World Tour, in which competitors who have won their spurs at national level can turn professional and participate in the international circuit. The World Tour consists of about 30 events in which the competitors race for prize money. The standard of equipment is exceptionally high, and this factor, coupled with the costs of globe trotting to far-flung locations, makes the world tour a pastime for the favoured few.

The funboard course is usually 'M' shaped. As the equipment is designed for slightly stronger airs, the course is designed so as to favour faster points of sailing, reaches, for example. Again, the start is on a beat: usually a kilometre upwind is sufficient to spread out the field in preparation for a series of broad reaches and a succession of carve gybes. In high winds some sailors take the gamble of sailing shorter slalom-type machines instead of the more traditional long funboard. Slalom boards can point to windward quite effectively in strong winds, and have unrivalled speed on the reaching legs.

Unless racing instructions say otherwise, higher wind racing is reserved for slalom. This is usually carried out near to the shore and as such attracts an enthusiastic following. Due to their smaller size and volume, slalom boards require a minimum of force 4 winds to be mobile. In these (and stronger) winds the slalom board's combination of straight line speed and gybing ability make it second to none.

Slalom courses, not surprisingly, are designed to bring out the best features of slalom boards. All the legs, therefore, are reaches, and all the turns are gybes. In a successful slalom, the competitors are arranged either into a series of leagues or into a double elimination knock-out table. The competitors sail in heats rather than in a fleet, usually eight at a time. In league slalom the top two sailors advance into the next league up and the bottom two move down a league. In knock-out the top four usually progress through to the next round. Though the start may be from either the beach or from the water, the latter is generally considered the more satisfactory. The course itself may vary a little depending on the location and conditions. Be sure to check the race

instructions prior to sailing. The norm of the downwind 'M' can incorporate a figure of eight around the last two buoys.

Certain events are not geared to any of the foregoing formats, yet you may still be called on to respect the rules and sailors' rights. Long-distance racing is a case in point. These are usualy run on a one-off basis, and the course is totally at the discretion of the race officer who will set the start and individual legs to fit in with the prevailing conditions.

There is also a funboard class hybrid called raceboard. The raceboard class has restricted sail sizes and only undertakes course races.

Apart from one-off crossings, island roundings, etc., class racing remains a popular pursuit. The original windsurfer still has a strong following in its own one design regattas, as has latterly the International Mistral Class Organization (I.M.C.O).

Slalom gybe mark

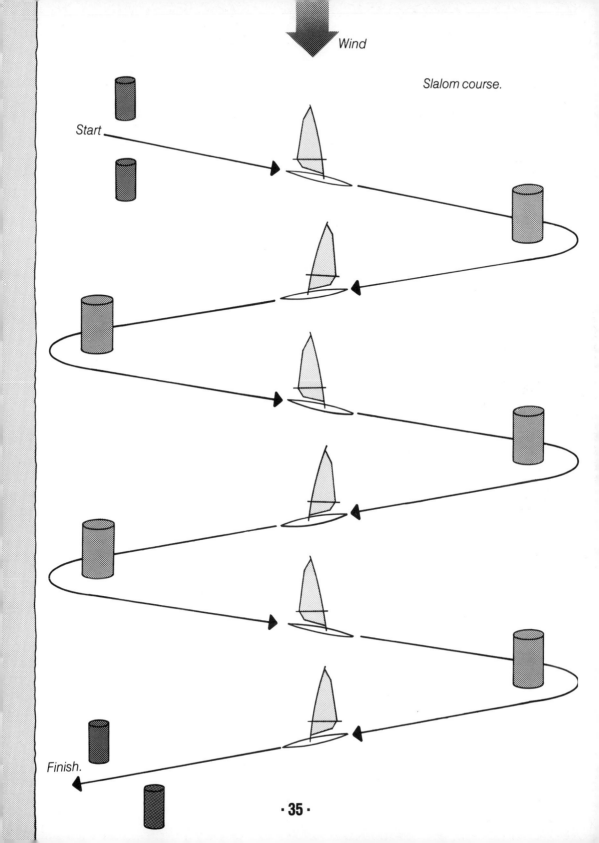

Wind

Slalom course.

Start

Finish.

Wavesailing competition

From the spectator's point of view there can be little doubt that wavesailing represents the most attractive side of windsurfing. There is no lack of high drama and spectacle with mast high waves being negotiated and leapt off by the intrepid sailor. A whole array of twists and contortions may accompany these aerial flights.

Competition waveriding began in Hawaii, but since then has been adopted in many other countries. Ideally, a wave contest should be set in cross-shore conditions, which allow the sailor to perform the greatest variety of manoeuvres both coming in and going out through the surf. Obviously most contests are set at known surf locations where there is likely to be strong wind – a minimum of force 3.5 is usually required. The stronger the wind, the more spectacular the action will be. If conditions are not perfect, the organizers may change the location, although most sailors can operate effectively in a wind ranging from cross onshore to cross offshore. The world's best venues are found in Australia and Hawaii, where the surf can combine with regular trade winds to give consistent conditions. Hookipa Beach Park, Maui, is the site for the most prestigious contests.

The nature of the waveriding contest clearly differs from racing, and placing the riders in order of merit is a matter of nice judgment. In general, judges base their decision on three categories – jumping, riding and transitions. A time limit is set bearing in mind the prevailing conditions. Heats are usually between five and ten minutes' duration. During the heat, only the best three jumps, rides and transitions count.

The classic mid-carve gybe shot. Note the upright torso yet forward and inward drive from both knees.

Off the lip.

There are no marks for artistic impression as such. Each manoeuvre is given a score out of 10. To arrive at an overall points total, the best three in each discipline are then multiplied – usually by 5 in riding, 3 in jumping and 2 in transitions. It soon becomes apparent that riding can count for as much as 50% of the final marks, so it is important to notch up a good score in that department.

A smart sailor will always start as far upwind as the competition area allows. Inevitably as the heat takes place the sailor will drift downwind, possibly out of the judging area, even. It certainly pays to perform the best manoeuvres in front of the judges. Marks are awarded on the basis of the degree of difficulty of a move and its successful completion. The riding points can be boosted by catching the largest wave and performing good turns and re-entries on it. Aerial re-entries and Gu screws score heavily. Jumping points are awarded on the basis of height and control while airborne.

WINDSURFING

Forward loop sequence

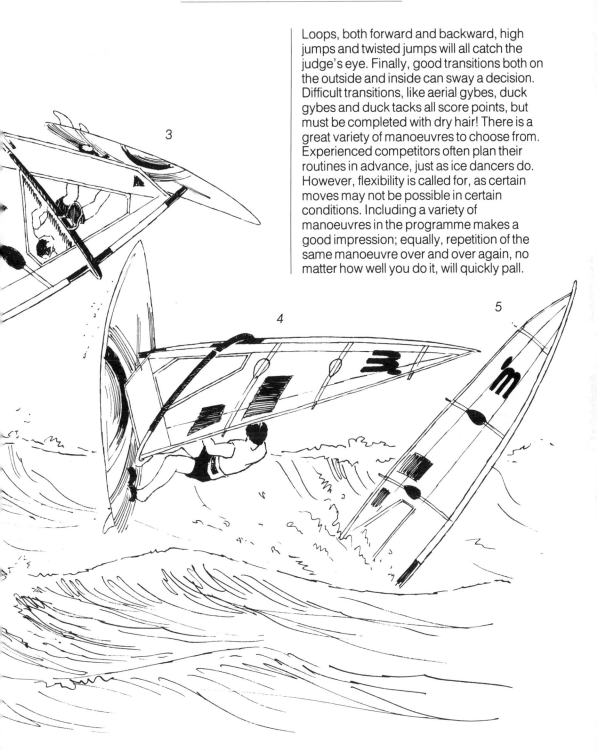

Loops, both forward and backward, high jumps and twisted jumps will all catch the judge's eye. Finally, good transitions both on the outside and inside can sway a decision. Difficult transitions, like aerial gybes, duck gybes and duck tacks all score points, but must be completed with dry hair! There is a great variety of manoeuvres to choose from. Experienced competitors often plan their routines in advance, just as ice dancers do. However, flexibility is called for, as certain moves may not be possible in certain conditions. Including a variety of manoeuvres in the programme makes a good impression; equally, repetition of the same manoeuvre over and over again, no matter how well you do it, will quickly pall.

WINDSURFING

Speedsailing

The concept of speedsailing is easy enough to grasp; the fastest sailor between two points wins the competition. A stiffish breeze is as much a prerequisite of speedsailing as of wavesailing. In fact boards built for speed, with their very narrow lines, demand winds in excess of force 4 to get onto the plane. Speed is dependent upon minimizing the wetted area, which accounts for the characteristic shape of speedboards.

The alignment of the speed course in relation to the wind is absolutely critical. The wind needs not oly to be strong, but constant in nature, undisturbed by buildings, trees or similar objects which might interfere with its free flow. The state of the water is also very important; to go fast and maintain any form of control the water must be as flat as possible.

Speedsailing requires very accurate timing, which is why the sport is governed by the World Speed Sailing Committee. This committee lays down certain rules and guidelines with which all recognized events must comply. Measurements of the course also have to be extremely accurate; for any form of ratified time the course must be exactly 500 metres in length. The transit

Sailor at speed

WINDSURFING

posts for start and finish must be independently surveyed to ascertain the set distance. In addition, video time-lapse cameras must be positioned at start and finish to ensure absolute accuracy. Lastly, at each recognized event a designated official must be present to supervise proceedings and see that fair play is done. Only then can the times be converted into knots and ratified.

Individual performances are carefully recorded, so as to formulate an overall ranking list. Each sailor will have his position registered, together with a personal time which can go forward onto a world ranking. The sailor at the head of the ranking list is the outright and undisputed world record holder.

In order to qualify as a new record the new time must exceed the old by a margin of 2%; this stipulation was introduced to remove any doubts about the accuracy of the timing. Even though timing is now exceptionally accurate, this rule still stands.

Suitable top-class locations for speedsailing are difficult to find, the difficulty being that where it is very windy the water is generally not flat. For this reason – its flat water – Sotavento, in the Canary island of Fuerteventura, is a favoured location. Speedsailing also takes place elsewhere, although often at a lower level. This has the advantage of allowing more people to compete, because it can be difficult to gain entry to ratified events, where precedence is naturally given to sailors with an established track record of fast times.

Start buoy

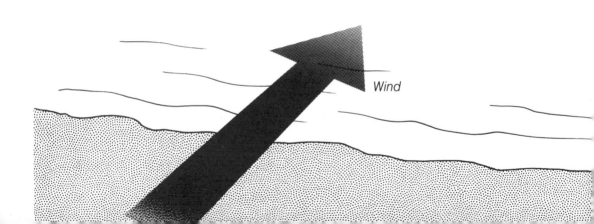

Wind

It stands to reason that shorter courses require more accurate timing, but unfortunately this is not always the case, as competitions like these are often run on a tight budget.

Recently, man-made courses have been constructed at considerable expense. These purpose-built canals or ditches are dug out and then flooded where there are strong winds – such as the south of France where the mistral blows. They are aligned so as to present the sail to the wind at the most favourable angle. The snag is that entry fees to these private trials are high (partly to pay for the official observer). Times in excess of 40 knots have been achieved in these clinical conditions.

In order to gain maximum speed over the measured distance it is essential to make your start coincide with a strong gust, which will provide the necessary acceleration to top speed. Provided that the wind is not affected by a bank, it is best to stay as close as possible to the windward side; this is where the flattest water will be found. If another sailor has just blasted off, leave some time for the wake to subside and the water to recover after being disturbed. A slight time lapse will also assure you of clean wind all along the course. If you have to sail back to the start, be sure to do so to leeward of any competitor making a run, otherwise he may not be too pleased with you! Lastly, use common sense at the finishing line, where there may well be a melee of boards, and where a careless sailor may well cause a collision.

Finish

Speed course

Beach 500 m

RULES AND RIGHTS OF WAY

The whole point of recreational sailing is that it is not encumbered by rules and regulations. Nevertheless, there are occasions when common sense, rather than a rigid set of rules, comes into play.

Collisions are at all costs to be avoided. It therefore pays to look ahead and make sure that the way is clear. Get into the habit of cultivating spatial awareness. Make a mental note of where there are obstacles, such as buoys or rocks.

As a general rule, the windsurfer should give way to any object that is considered less manoeuverable. Surfers, canoeists and (above all) swimmers fall into this category. Any powdered craft, on the other hand, *should* give way to the windsurfer; this includes jet skis, launches and motorboats of any description. Do not assume, though, that because you have seen the powered vessel, its captain has seen you! Larger ocean-going boats, although powered, are not very manoeuverable, so use foresight and common sense in steering clear of them.

As for other windsurfers, the basic 'port and starboard' rule applies; if sailors are on opposite tacks, the sailor on the starboard tack has right of way and the port tack sailor must stay clear. Remember that when your right hand is nearest the mast you are on starboard tack, if it's the left hand, you are on a port tack. If both sailors are on the same tack, then the craft running free should give way; the sailor on a broad reach should give way to a sailor to windward who is on a tighter heading.

Racing rules

When racing, knowledge of the rules is crucial, since without it even the best sailor may lose on a technicality. As might be expected, the rules derive from yacht racing, in particular the International Yacht Racing Union.

The rule most invoked is number 36, regarding port and starboard priority. In a race situation a cry of 'starboard' means that the port tacked sailor is obliged to give way.

Another general rule is that the windward craft must keep clear of the leeward craft. This rule is very useful on a reach where a leeward board can force an overtaking windward rival up to wind to a point where he may slow to a standstill. While executing this move, you run the risk of other competitors

Here the world's most famous windsurfer, Robby Naish (US IIII) takes on Paulo Rista (I 222) at a wave contest.

WINDSURFING

Rules and rights of way.

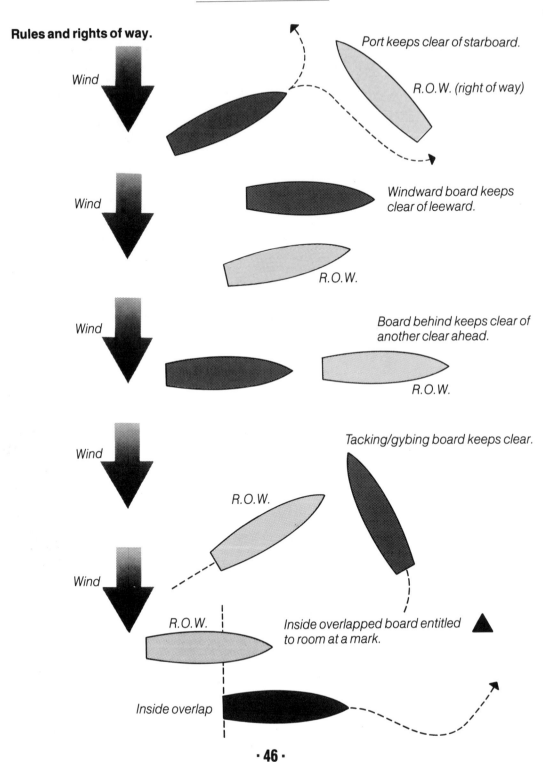

Wind

Port keeps clear of starboard.

R.O.W. (right of way)

Wind

Windward board keeps clear of leeward.

R.O.W.

Wind

Board behind keeps clear of another clear ahead.

R.O.W.

Wind

Tacking/gybing board keeps clear.

R.O.W.

Wind

R.O.W.

Inside overlapped board entitled to room at a mark.

Inside overlap

slipping past you downwind.

The overlap rule may be used to gain water at a mark. If you can gain an overlap of your mast to the other's beam outside of two board lengths from the mark, then you can shout for water at the mark; this means that if you are inside and upwind, you can force the other craft to go exceptionally wide at the mark. In all circumstances bar this (where the overlap rule applies) the overtaking sailor must keep clear of the opposition.

The port/starboard and windward rules also apply at the start, so it is important not to get caught out at this critical stage. A good race officer will always try and set the line with a slight port bias. Unless the bias is massively to port, always cross the line on starboard, otherwise you have no rights at all.

Obviously, these basic rules are merely a selection from the text of the I.Y.R.U. rule book, which should be closely studied, in view of the complicated scenarios that sometimes occur when racing. Any infringement of the rules can be nullified by completing a 720 degree turn, a penalty that costs both time and placing. The alternative to paying this penalty is gracious retirement, or the prospect of facing a protest at the end of the race. Slalom racing is not subject to I.Y.R.U. rules: here it is every man for himself!

Surf sailing

The I.Y.R.U. rules also don't count in surf locations: even rules regarding port and starboard tend to be ignored. There is a common consensus, though, that the sailor going out through the waves has right of way over the sailor coming in, or riding the wave. This makes sense, because the incoming rider has more control and ability to change direction.

If there are two or more sailors on the same wave, then the one who is furthest upwind has control. If he decides to ride downwind, then the other sailors must respect this decision and keep clear.

It is not good form to make a transition onto a wave purely to gain the upwind position. If the wave has already formed, and a sailor gybes onto it upwind of others, he has no rights. In a roundabout way this leads on to another rule, that the sailor who catches the wave first has priority. A sailor cannot come onto the wave from behind and expect any water.

Finally, the sailor nearest the most critical part of the wave has priority. This rule basically gives a sailor who is trying to work the most powerful part of the wave freedom to do so. Often novice wavesailors do not use the full power of the wave, riding the shallower and more forgiving sections. If this rule is applied, it means that expert sailors can ride along the wave with the breaking section.

TECHNIQUE

BEGINNER'S TECHNIQUES

Anyone of any age with reasonable balance and coordination can learn to windsurf. Needles to say, it is not just a matter of getting onto the board and sailing away. Inevitably you will flounder and struggle for a while, but the learning process can be shortened if the steps involved are analysed and understood beforehand.

Rigging up

Setting up the rig is a simple process, and should generally take 15 to 20 minutes if done methodically. It is a mistake to try to do this job in too much of a hurry. A poorly rigged sail will only have to be re-rigged after a spell of unsatisfactory sailing.

The first thing to do is to slip the mast up the luff sleeve of the sail, and then attach the head, or turban. Insert the mast foot or extension into the base of the mast and apply a hint of downhaul, preferably using a built-in pulley system. Any sail with a floating adjustable head will need it secured to a point so that when the sail is eventually fully downhauled the tack eyelet is about an inch from its cleat.

Attach the boom securely to the mast anywhere from chest to shoulder level,

depending on where you want it. A clamping front boom end is by far the best method of securing mast to boom. Now transfer your attention to the rear boom end. Outhaul the sail roughly to its known boom length, using any integral rear boom pulleys if you have them. Now back to the downhaul for a good hard pull. Most modern sails require a lot of downhaul tension. Pulleys on the mast foot are essential to gain a 5:1 or 6:1 ratio. Watch out for rope burn when exerting downhaul pressure. To make tensioning easier, sit down and place one foot on the base of the mast foot. The best plan is simultaneously to push with your foot and pull the line.

Insert the foot batten and any other battens into their respective pockets if they are not in them already. Tension all battens up so that any vertical wrinkles along the pockets disappear.

Finally, take time to tune the sail to the prevailing conditions before going onto the water. Raise the rig on the shoreline. If the sail feels a little overpowered, tension the downhaul and outhaul a bit more. If the sail is flat as a board, it will feel twitchy and powerless. In this case, release some of the outhaul and downhaul tension.

Rigging errors are common, and easy to spot. The most common error is lack of downhaul tension, which affects the sail's handling very adversely. Horizontal creases when under power are also a giveaway. Check that the luff in the boom cut out area is tight. It's worth noting that it is difficult to over downhaul a modern sail. A sail with insufficient outhaul will develop vertical head to foot creases. The sail will feel very sluggish as it will create a lot of drag in use. Less critically, level creases in the luff area usually mean that the mast is the wrong stiffness, or that its bend characteristics are not compatible with the sail. Check again for any batten pocket wrinkles.

Derigging is simply a reversal of the rigging up procedure. It is important not to release the outhaul tension before slacking off the downhaul, otherwise the mast will try and straighten itself, seriously distorting the luff area of the sail in the process.

Carrying board and rig

Long boards are often cumbersome to get to the water's edge. It therefore makes sense first to take the board and then return for the rig: don't take the rig first, or it might blow onto the water and drift away. (Take care when carrying your gear over shingle or stones. Carelessness in doing so could seriously damage your wealth.)

Lay the board across the rig and approach from the upwind side.

The hull can be transported by using the daggerboard slot or mast track as a firm place to grip and balancing it roughly about its central point. For those of slighter build the assistance of a friend will be useful, especially if it is windy. Always stand to windward of the rig with the mast nearest to you. It should be easy to lift the rig by means of the mast and boom, whereupon the wind will flow under the sail, making it lighter.

Most funboards, once on the beach, can be transported as one unit. First, position the board across the wind. Then, staying upwind of the rig, position the mast so that it lies to the back of the board. Now hold one of the windward footstraps and the boom. As you lift the board the wind should blow under the hull and rig, helping you on your way.

As you progress onto smaller boards, the transportation problems become easier. Waveboards and their rigs can often be seen being transported on top of the head. Don't make the mistake of trying this trick with a heavier board, or you may damage your spine.

Lift the board with the front footstrap and the top of the boom, so that the wind blows under the hull and sail.

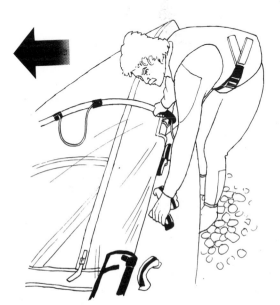

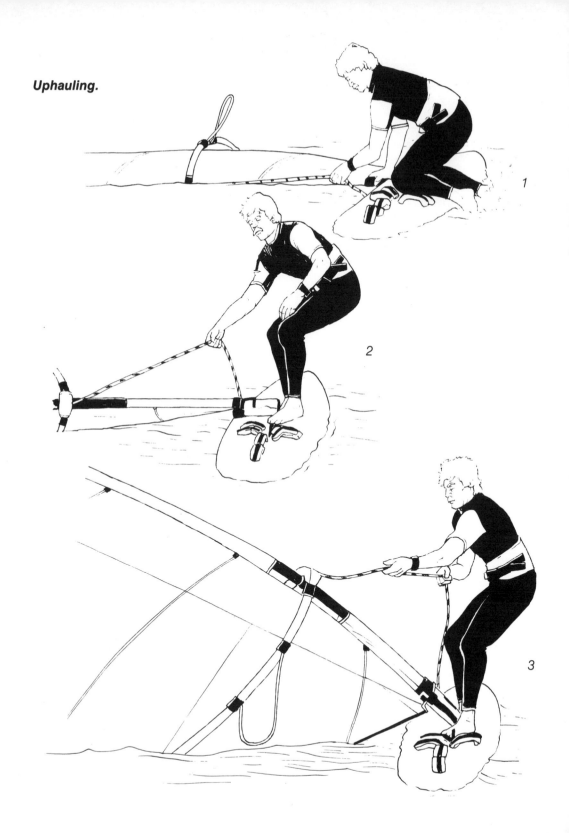

Uphauling.

1

2

3

To uphaul the rig place the board in the water, allowing enough depth so that when you fall off (as you certainly will, and frequently) you won't hit the bottom. To get aboard, approach the hull from the windward side; the sail should be downwind of the board. Climb out of the water, and onto the board near the mastfoot area, which is the most buoyant and stable part of the board. Kneel down astride the mastfoot to get better balance.

If you take the uphaul rope with the front hand it will act as a counterweight against which you can lean to help your balance. Using the uphaul as an aid, straighten yourself up gradually, keeping your knees bent and back straight; your lower centre of gravity will make balancing easier. Place your feet about a shoulder-width apart, equidistant about the mastfoot. By holding the uphaul you can keep the rig at approximately 90° to the hull by exerting left and right foot pressure.

To lift the sail, straighten your legs and back while pulling the uphaul. To start with, this will be difficult, owing to the weight of water lying on the sail. As the water drains off, continue straightening your legs while taking in the uphaul with a hand-over-hand motion. It gets easier as water drains off the sail and out of the luff tube. A common error made by learners is not to anticipate the progressive ease of lifting the sail, and to pull too hard for too long: result – a back flop into the water, followed by the sail! The sail should now be completely free of the water. Let the sail flap freely in the breeze. The free-flying sail is an important indicator of the wind direction. Transfer one or both hands to hold the mast below the boom. This position should feel relaxed and stable. It should be returned to in any moment of doubt, and should be thought of as a netural, secure position, balanced and ready for action, but not yet moving forward.

Start position

The secure position

The author chop hopping at Spreckellsville, Maui.

Sailing away

Having mastered the secure position it is now time for some forward motion and the transition to the sailing position. When composed, release your rear hand from the secure position. Keeping the mast in its original plane, move both feet back. Your front foot should be adjacent to the mastfoot and pointing slightly forward and your rear foot at a comfortable stride back and over the daggerboard casing. This is the start position. Turn to look in the direction of your intended goal. Then pull the rig to a balance point to windward, near to your front shoulder. At the balance point the rig should feel almost weightless.

In one swift movement rest your rear or sheeting hand on the boom. The sail will immediately start to power up. As it does so, the board will move forward. If it feels comfortable you can place your front hand on the mastward end of the boom. Relocate your body weight onto the rear foot to counterbalance any pull from the rig. You should now be comfortable moving forward in the recognized 'sailing position'.

Sailing position

Steering

With a little practice it doesn't take long to feel comfortable and at ease in the sailing position. The next priority is steering, either up towards the wind, which is called 'heading up', or down away from the wind, known as 'bearing away'. Heading up is the easier of the two manoeuvres. From the sailing position, on a reach, you start to head up by tilting the rig aft. As you do so, sheet in harder with the back hand and move your weight aft to aid the turn. The nose of the board will head up towards the wind. To stop the turning movement, simply tilt the mast back towards its original position.

To start bearing away, tilt the mast forward and once again sheet in. Once the board starts to react, sheet out a touch and reposition your weight forwards. By tilting the rig at the board you will stop turning and sail in a straight line.

Left

Heading up: turning the board into the eye of the wind. Tilt the rig backwards and sheet in with your sail hand. As the pressure grows on the sail, move your rear foot back to help balance. When you are pointing in the right direction, tilt the rig forwards again.

Right

Bearing away: turning the board away from the eye of the wind. Tilt the rig forwards and sheet in. Move your front foot forwards as the wind acts on the front of the sail and sheet out. When you are moving in the right direction, tilt the rig back again.

WINDSURFING

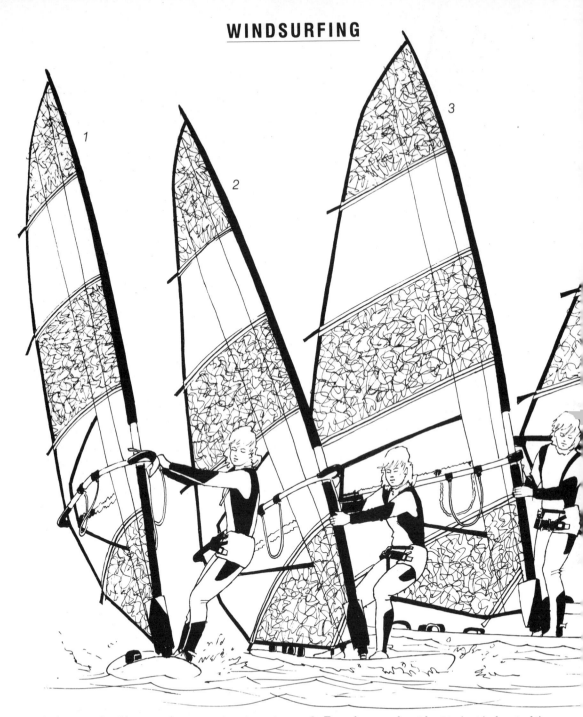

1 Approach with enough momentum to get you through the turn. Begin to lean back and sheet in slightly.

2 Transfer your front foot to just in front of the mast and your front hand to the mast below the boom. Keep the rig angled back.

Tacking

In order to get back to the point where you started, you need to be able to turn the board around. This 180° turn around is known as the (upwind) or (downwind) tack or gybe.

Going upwind to tack is the simpler of the two manoeuvres. Tacking really comes into its own when the sailor wishes to arrive at a point which is directly upwind. As it is impossible to sail dead upwind, you have to sail a series of zig-zags known as close hauls, changing tack and zig-zagging to windward.

The most basic tack is achieved from the secure position. Tilt the mast towards the tail of the board: this makes the nose of the board turn towards the eye of the wind. Keep leaning the rig aft until the board is head to wind. At this point, step smartly around the mast, staying as close as possible to the mast foot, so as not to upset the board's equilibrium. Continue to tilt the mast and rig in a similar direction until the board has spun a complete 180°. Reassume a new secure position on the new tack.

Once the basic concept is grasped, you can then speed up the tacking process. You will observe that the harder you sheet in, and the further you position your weight aft, the faster the turn. From a sailing position you can hop round the mast and, with good timing, immediately take the new boom to bear away in a new sailing position.

3 When the board slows down and turns head to wind (or preferably just after) bring your back foot up to join your front foot, and your back hand up to join your front hand on the mast.

4 Reach for the boom with what was your front hand and bring the sail across your body and sheet in.

5 You're away on the new tack.

Gybing

From a sailing position, tilt the mast forward and slightly to windward by extending the leading arm as for bearing away. As the nose of the board turns away from the wind continue this steering motion, sheeting out a little as you point further downwind. As you approach a dead downwind point of sailing, known as a run, move your front foot aft to stand on either side of the board's centreline near the daggerboard casing.

In order to continue the turn and gybe the sail, take your rear hand from the boom to grasp the mast. With the help of the wind, swing the sail over the bows of the board. For the first few attempts it is a good idea to reassume the start position before setting off on the new tack.

It should not take the enthusiastic learner too long to master the basic gybe. It is not, however, the most efficient way of turning a flat board downwind. The flare gybe offers a quicker transition that also loses less ground downwind. It is a very useful manoeuvre in progressive long board sailing, and certainly in longboard racing.

The rig operation in such a gybe is very similar in motion to the standard gybe, but more exaggerated in effect. To turn tightly, push the daggerboard down fully. Get well back on the board, and from a reach depress the windward rail, whereupon the board will spin on its axis. For the flare gybe better balance and timing is required than for the conventional longboard gybe.

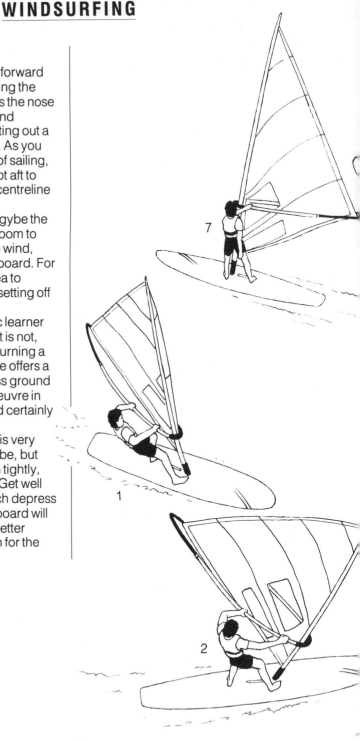

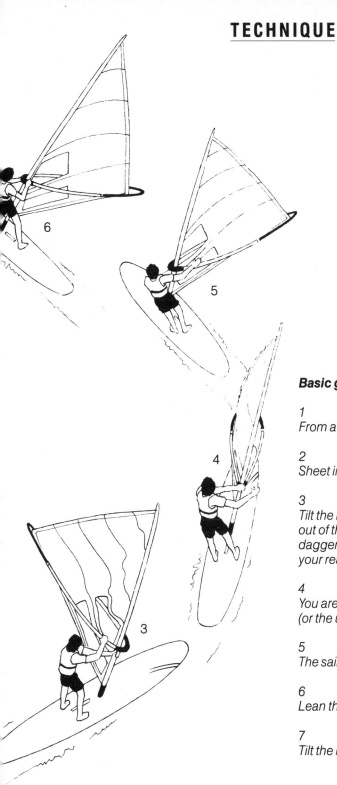

Basic gybing.

1
From a beam reach, bear away.

2
Sheet in a little with the sail hand.

3
Tilt the mast sideways so that the board turns out of the wind. Position feet either side of the daggerboard casing. Grasp the mast with your rear hand.

4
You are now on a run. Grasp the boom front (or the uphaul).

5
The sail swings round over the bow.

6
Lean the sail into the wind.

7
Tilt the mast forward and sheet in.

WINDSURFING

Beach start

The windsurfer who has mastered the art of beach starting has a distinct advantage over the windsurfer who can only uphaul. Uphauling can be a tedious and exhausting business, especially in high winds and rough water. Not only is it more convenient, it is much more stylish to be able to step onto the board straight from the beach.

Ideally, a force two to three wind is require for first attempts at beach starting. Make sure the daggerboard is retracted, so that the board can manoeuvre more freely about the fin. Position the board in the shallows, about knee deep, directly across the wind. Standing to windward of the board, hold the boom in the sailing position. To maintain the board's position, use mastfoot pressure only: pushing down through the mastfoot will bear the board away, whereas pulling back through the mastfoot will make the board luff up.

Raise the rig slightly so as to get nearer to the board close to the footstraps. Lift your back foot onto the board, directly on its centreline. To generate lift, bear away and extend your front arm to present the sail to the wind. Control any undue pull of the sail by sheeting in or out with the back hand. As you extend both arms, hop aboard with your front foot. If you time this movement to coincide with a gust, the wind will do more of the work for you.

Once safely aboard, power up the sail straight into the sailing position. It may be necessary to bear away slightly to stop the board heading into the wind. Needless to say, the long board beach start is readily adaptable to short-board sailing once you progress that far.

1
Control the board's position with your front hand on the mast and the back hand on the boom.

2
With the board on a reach and both hands on the boom, put your back foot across the centreline.

3
Extend the arms to get the rig forward and upright.

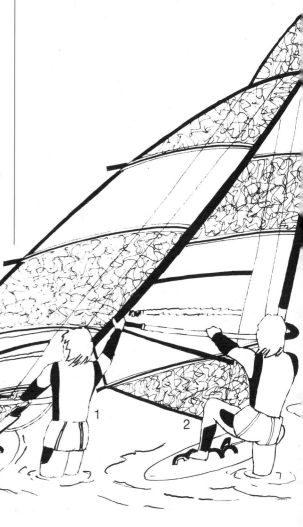

4
The hips are thrust forwards over the bent leg.

5
Lever down on the boom to raise the front leg, and place the front foot over the centreline.

SAFETY

Equipment breakage is a serious matter, so always check your gear before going on the water. Lines are very susceptible to wear, so make a careful check, and replace worn ones. The universal joint is also subject to a great deal of wear and tear, so fitting a webbing U.J. saver is a good idea; even if it snaps far offshore you will still be able to get back.

Try not to sail for extended periods without a break. It's easy to become tired, especially if you haven't mastered the use of the harness. If you drift downwind it may become impossible to sail back to your original launch site in an exhausted condition.

Lastly, take note of weather conditions before you go afloat. Always check the weather report as a matter of course, and be aware that weather conditions can change rapidly. Unless very experienced, never sail in an offshore wind. Tell someone where you intend to be sailing, and how long you expect to be gone. Many a novice ventures out in conditions way beyond his capabilities. **If in doubt, don't go out!** Don't be afraid to ask fellow sailors for advice about the best sail size to use, or about tides and currents. Knowledge of local conditions is an indispensable asset to any sailor, and not just the windsurfer.

If you get into difficulties, it may be possible to attract the attention of another sailor who can give you a tow to safety. Since voices do not carry very well on a windy day at sea, make you intentions clear by using the international distress signal. Sit astride your board and move both arms up and down mimicking a flying action; if someone spots you they should come to your assistance.

If the situation is not desperate, and you are close to the shore, a self-rescue may be feasible, but don't embark on this operation and then change your mind half-way through it. Knowledge of the technique of self-rescue is essential for anyone who puts out to sea – or indeed inland waters – on a board. It is usually in the earlier stages of windsurfing that you might need to put it into practice. The object of the exercise is to be able to paddle the board to safety with the rig stowed away beneath you.

First, sit on the board with your back to the wind. Unplug the mastfoot and work along the sail's foot, removing any battens. Untie the outhaul and remove any battens in the leech. Roll the sail in tightly towards the mast, laying the boom towards the mast tip. Use the uphaul and outhaul lines to secure the package. Position the stowed rig under your body, then lie on top of it to paddle ashore.

If you are in a very tight situation, or you are obviously making no headway, don't be afraid to ditch the rig and paddle the hull ashore. But whatever you do, and however well you can swim, do not in any circumstances leave the board and make a break for it!

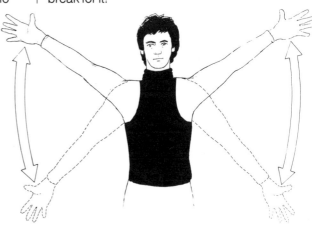

Up-and-down motion of the arms, sitting astride the board, a universally recognised distress signal.

TECHNIQUE

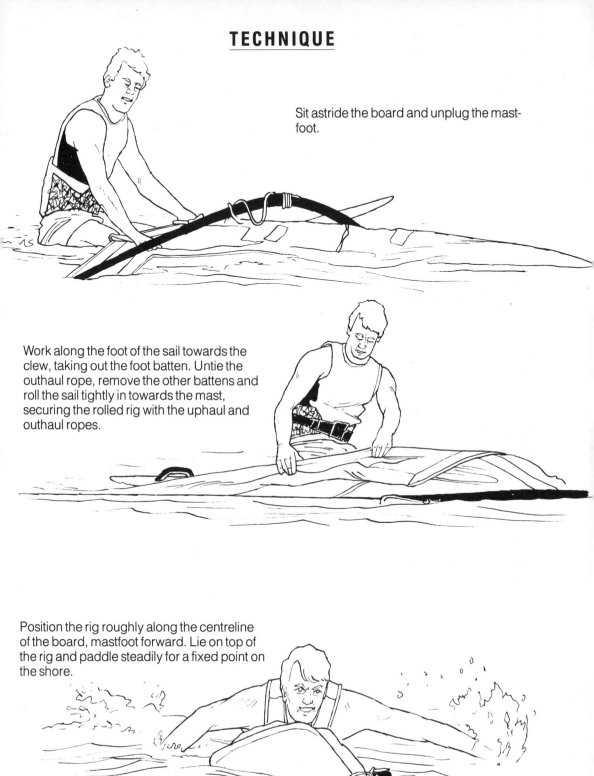

Sit astride the board and unplug the mast-foot.

Work along the foot of the sail towards the clew, taking out the foot batten. Untie the outhaul rope, remove the other battens and roll the sail tightly in towards the mast, securing the rolled rig with the uphaul and outhaul ropes.

Position the rig roughly along the centreline of the board, mastfoot forward. Lie on top of the rig and paddle steadily for a fixed point on the shore.

WINDSURFING

Bjorn Dunkerbeck, probably windsurfing's most versatile competitor, putting a course board through its paces.

BEAUFORT SCALE OF WIND FORCE

Beaufort No	General Description	Sea criterion	Landsman's Criterion	Limits of * velocity in knots
0	Calm	Sea like a mirror	Calm; smoke rises vertically	Less than 1
1	Light air	Ripples with the appearance of scales are formed, but without foam crests.	Direction of wind shown by smoke drift but not by wind vanes.	1 to 3
2	Light breeze	Small wavelets, still short but more pronounced. Crests have a glassy appearance and do not have break.	Wind felt on face; leaves rustle; ordinary vane moved by wind.	4 to 6
3	Gentle breeze	Large wavelets. Crests begin to break. Foam of glassy appearance. Perhaps scattered white horses.	Leaves and small twigs in constant motion. Wind extends light flags.	7 to 10
4	Moderate breeze	Small waves becoming longer, fairly frequent white horses.	Raises dust and loose paper; small branches are moved.	11 to 16
5	Fresh breeze	Moderate waves, taking more pronounced long form; many white horses are formed. Chances of some spray.	Small trees in leaf begin to sway. Crested wavelets form on inland waters.	17 to 21
6	Strong breeze	Large waves begin to form; the white foam crests are more extensive everywhere. Probably some spray.	Large branches in motion; whistling heard in telegraph wires, umbrellas used with difficulty.	22 to 27
7	Near gale	Sea heaps up and white foam from breaking waves begins to be blown in streaks along the direction of the wind.	Whole trees in motion; inconvenience felt when walking against wind.	28 to 33
8	Gale	Moderately high waves of greater length; edges of crests begin to break into spin-drift. The foam is blown in well-marked streaks along the direction of the wind.	Breaks twigs off trees; generally impedes progress.	34 to 40

INTERMEDIATE TECHNIQUES

Funboard sailing

Funboard sailing relies on the idea of using a planing hull to its maximum potential. Nevertheless, knowledge of flatboard techniques is required if the aspiring funboarder is to make good progress in his chosen conditions, that is to say, in winds in excess of force 3 or 4. The mastery of funboarding technique will inevitably lead to many a spill, as this or that manoeuvre is attempted – it is only by sailing to the edge of your capability that you can progress.

The funboarder should concentrate first on developing a solid stance, and then progress to use of the harness, to conserve energy and maintain pressure on the mastfoot. The key to board speed and instant acceleration is mastfoot pressure. Pushing your weight down through the mastfoot levels the board and trims it whilst planing. Once on the plane, this pressure will then enable you to move back on the board and into the footstraps. It is at this point that footsteering becomes possible.

Poor stance is responsible for many funboarding errors. Try to look where you're going. If your head is pointing in the right direction it will help align your shoulders correctly, relative to the sail. A quick glance over the shoulder will tell you whether there are other water users in the vicinity.

Both arms should be very slightly bent when on a close reach. If a gust hits you, respond by extending both arms fully to hold the power of the sail comfortably. If you are fully powered up and anticipate a gust, keep your front arm straight. This will minimise the rig's pull on the arm muscles. Both hands should be positioned at an equal distance from the rig's balance point: a shoulder-width apart is about right. Whether the grip of the leading hand is overhand or underhand is a matter for personal preference, but the back hand grip should certainly be overhand.

In funboarding, as indeed in all forms of windsurfing, it is best to keep the rig as upright as possible at all times – the whole sail area is then presented to the wind. Use your lower torso as a counterbalance against gusts in keeping the rig upright. When the wind drops and lulls occur, shift your hips in and upwards; in the gusts, move them out to take the strain of the additional rig pull.

Your legs should be slightly bent in order to act as shock absorbers when the ride gets bumpy, as it certainly will over undulating water. Your feet should be at a comfortable distance apart. The novice's frog-like stance, with feet and hands wide apart, is inefficient, and inappropriate for funboard sailing.

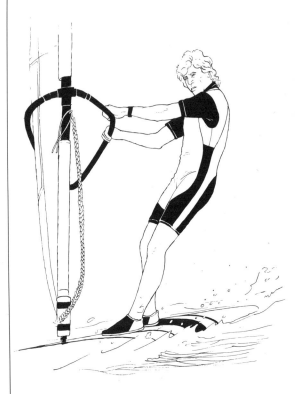

Funboard stance.

Harness use

The harness is surely the windsurfer's best friend when sailing in moderate to high winds. Not only does it take the strain off the arms, particularly forearms and biceps, but it is a great asset in trimming the board via the mastfoot, making sailing both faster and more efficient.

It is important to set up the lines correctly. The aim here should be to set them in a position so that when you are hooked in you can assume a normal sailing stance. Hold the rig on the beach as if you were sailing, hands shoulder-width apart. When you are in a comfortable position, move both hands together. If the rig is still stable you should arrive at the boom's balance point. Attach the harness line heads at an equal distance on either side of this balance point, about a shoulder-width apart. Now alter the harness line length to a point where both arms are slightly bent, when you are hooked in. It is possible to check the line's position by releasing both hands when hooked in. The harness should hold the rig's pull and not slew off at an angle. Practise hooking in and out on dry land. You will find that the line can be swung to and fro by twitching the rig. Practise catching the line on the hook when it is at its nearest point; a violent swing is unnecessary, and will also disturb your own balance.

In certain circumstances it is best to unhook. Unhooking in advance of a very strong gust can prevent an in-harness catapult. If you start to feel uncontrollably overpowered, free the lines until you feel comfortable again. Unless you are attempting a very advanced one-handed or tail grab, you should always be unhooked when jumping to maintain maximum control while in flight.

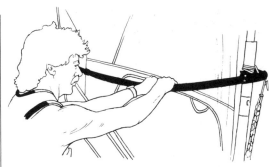

Hold the rig on the beach with your hands a shoulder width apart. Move them together; where they meet should be the point of balance for the boom.

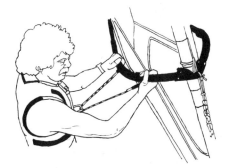

Attach the two ends of the line equidistant from the balance point, a shoulder width apart. The lines should be short enough so that your arms are slightly bent when hooked in and sailing.

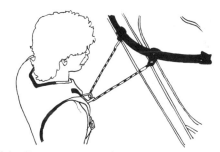

If the lines are correctly positioned, you should be able to take your hands off the boom and take the weight of the rig on your body without it twisting away.

Footstrap use

Always try to get back into the footstraps at the earliest possible opportunity. You are then in a position to footsteer, and also respond to gusts in a positive manner.

If there's insufficient wind you will find it impossible to step back on the board without the tail sinking, so planing conc ons are necessary for footstrap use. To begin with, use the front or training set of footstraps, as they are the easiest to get into. Make sure that you are fully in control and that you have good board speed: the faster you're going, the easier it is to move back. Take the weight off your feet by redistributing it through the mastfoot. The harness should help here. As you move back, the board should stay level and steady on its course. If you have too little pressure on the mastfoot the board may luff up into the wind. Place your front foot first into the windward front strap and then your rear foot into the foremost of the central back straps. Only after familiarising yourself with the training straps should you then attempt to use the rear straps.

Footstrap use. If you try to move into the straps before the board has picked up speed, you may sink the tail and spin into the wind. Hold the rig forward to encourage the board to accelerate as you move back.

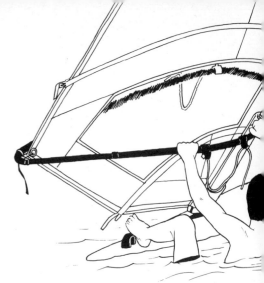

Keeping the rig well out of the water to stop the boom from catching, rest the heel of the back foot on the centreline; looking for a gust of wind in light conditions, prepare to spring with an explosive arm extension.

Waterstart

Uphauling a windsurfer sail in winds in excess of force four is not an easy task. The object of the waterstart is to let the wind do the work for you. If the sail is presented correctly to the wind it should physically lift you from the water and straight aboard. Waterstarting opens up the world of higher wind sailing, particular for the shorter boards, which have insufficient volume to allow conventional uphauling.

The best conditions for learning are winds of force 3 or 4, using a board which can be easily uphauled should you need to. The trickiest part to master is aligning the rig correctly for the start. Practice in shallow water is the best idea: look upon the manoeuvre as a sort of deep-water beach start.

The sail must be positioned in such a way that the wind can blow under the mast and help lift it clear of the water. This is not as easy as it sounds, as the rig can fall into some really awkward positions. Again, trial and error in the shallows should give you a good idea of the problems and the solutions –

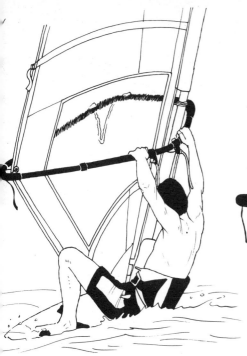

Kick hard with the front leg which remains in the water until the last moment. Come up under the boom. Pump the sail if necessary for greater lift.

As the front foot comes up onto the board, keep the back leg bent to lower the centre of gravity.

trying to figure things out in deep water can be frustrating as well as very uncomfortable. You may find it easier to swim the rig around so that it is to windward of the board on a close reach. Make sure that both the sail and board are pointing in the direction you want to travel. To fly the sail, work along from the mast tip, lifting as you go; the wind should flow under the sail and help it up. When the rig is completely free, grasp the boom as if in a sailing position. Work your way towards the tail of the board, using mastfoot pressure through the boom; this will have the effect of bearing the board away onto a broad reach, ready for the start itself.

Maintain mastfoot pressure so as to prevent luffing up, then lift your back foot onto the board, resting your heel on the hull's imaginary centreline, just forward of the rear straps. To generate lift, extend both arms, so that you present as much sail to the wind as

possible. Simultaneously try to project yourself out of the water with all your strength. As you begin to clear the water, with both arms fully extended, you may find that a sharp kick with your front foot may give that extra drive to get yourself right out of the water. Stay on a broad reach until the board has levelled out and you are in complete control.

In stronger airs you will need to modify the technique slightly. As the wind rises, you can get away with presenting less and less sail area to it, and still get sufficient lift. There comes a point where you can start with one foot, or both feet, in the straps, which helps control and prevents a rapid catapult as you burst out of the water.

Dunkerbeck casually illustrates the carved duck gybe. Foot position and body inclination maintain the board's arc.

Carve gybe

The carve gybe is a fully planing 180°
downwind turn. Good execution of this
manoeuvre involves all the skills of board and
timing. The mark of a good carve gybe is that
the speed of exit is similar to the speed of
entry. Some boards will carve this classic
funboard turn better than others. Though it is
possible to carve even the longest
funboards, they tend to need coaxing round
the turn a little, especially if they have sharp
rails. On the other hand, an out-and-out
waveboard will bank around like a waterskier
cutting a turn.

Ideal learning conditions are a good force
4 and flat water. Choppy water will slow any
board down and even cause some boards to
trip or bounce out. If attempting to carve on a
long funboard, the daggerboard must be
retracted and the mastfoot near the back of
the track. From a reach, look for an area of
flat water in which to execute your turn. Bear
away to gain maximum speed and unhook
from the harness. As you enter a broad
reach, take your rear foot out of its strap and
place it towrds the leeward rail. Start by
pressuring the rail and bending both knees to
drive the board through the turn.

As the board turns, drive the knees
forward, keeping the torso upright and your
weight on the mastfoot. Footsteer the board
past the run position and towards a new tack.
Just as the moment when the rig comes clew
first, release your back hand. If you continue
to carve, your front hand will act as a pivot

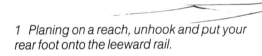

1 *Planing on a reach, unhook and put your
rear foot onto the leeward rail.*

2 *Lean inwards and forwards. Put pressure
on the rail.*

3 *Continue to lean gradually into the turn.*

about which the rig will flip, aided by the wind. As the rig flips, be ready to take the other side of the boom with your other hand. Sheet in the sail, and finally change over your feet to sail off on a new reach.

Timing is the key to the whole exercise. If the rig change is too early or late, you will take a bath! A common mistake is to change the feet mid-gybe; this only causes the board to break from its arc and spin off on an uncontrollable run. In the early stages you shouldn't worry too much about the tightness of the arc; the longer turn is more forgiving of errors.

Mastery of the carve gybe is the key to other short-board transitions. A useful refinement is the act of stroking the water on the inside of the turn, in the middle of the gybe. Besides looking good, this can help commit the sailor to the arc, particularly when the board is prone to break free from the turn in strong winds.

5 Cross the rear hand over to grasp the boom as it comes around.

4 Passing through the downwind position, remove the rear hand ready for the rig change.

6 Put the power on for the new reach and reposition the feet.

Duck gybe

In the early days of funboarding the duck gybe was a transition that only the expert was capable of executing. Now, with more understanding of windsurfing principles and more user-friendly equipment, it is within the grasp of anyone who can carve gybe.

The duck gybe is in many respects similar to the carve gybe; in both manoeuvres the idea is to enter at speed and steer the board through the turn. The only difference is that in the duck gybe you duck under the sail in mid-carve and recapture the new boom to power out of the turn.

Start the turn in exactly the same way as the carve gybe. At an early stage of the arc begin the rig change. Cross the front hand over to the back of the boom and release the back hand. Maintaining the carve, pass under the swooping sail. It is important to take the new boom in front of its balance point. This may entail throwing the rear boom end back over your shoulder as you release it. With the front hand in position, power up the sail to complete the turn; only as you exit the turn should you change over your feet onto the new tack. There are many pitfalls to avoid; resist the temptation to slow down on entry or else the board will stop in mid-turn. Practise the rig change, especially the throwing, on dry land to get an idea of the timing involved. Always maintain a low centre of gravity, especially when travelling under the sail or the mast is likely to swing down and hit water during the rig change and cause a dramatic catapult.

TECHNIQUE

1
Carve off the wind as if entering a normal
carve gybe.

2
Cross the front hand over to the rear boom
end and release the back hand.

3
Duck under the sail as it swings around and
throw the rig back over your shoulder to take
hold of the new boom as close to the mast as
possible.

4
Power up the sail first with the front and then
the back hand.

Chop jumping

There is no doubt that wave jumping is the most visually appealing aspect of windsurfing. It is an accomplishment that most windsurfers dream of attempting. In fact, it is not as difficult as it may at first appear to be.

The most elementary form of jump, and the best starting point, is the chop hop. Successful chop jumping requires accurate timing without the hazards of flying high. The secret is to gain as much speed as possible prior to take-off. It's best to travel on a reach and be fully planing. Ideally, a force 4 and a board under 3 metres in length are called for. The beauty of a chop jump is that you don't need a large wave; a wavelet, or even a piece of chop on inland water will suffice.

Look well ahead for the take-off ramp and unhook from the harness well before you hit it. As the nose of the board goes up the ramp, pull up on the boom and with your front foot. Time sheeting in and raising your rear leg to coincide with the tail of the board leaving the ramp. Good jumping is all about control while airborne. To gain maximum lift, remain sheeted in during the whole flight. It's possible to gain further lift by showing the underside of the board to the wind. To level out and maintain control, raise the back leg up and to windward. As your time in the air is very short, you must concentrate on landing. The safest landing, at least in the early stages, is tail-first. As the board approaches the water, extend the back leg and lean back a little to prevent an instant catapult on landing.

With only a little practice your jumping co-ordination should improve, and you should soon achieve greater height. With mastery of the chop jump, the basic techniques can then be applied to other aerial manoeuvres. You will find that the principle of the long, flat jump is the same.

Whether you ever reach the skill level of wave jumping or entering races, or simply enjoy the particularly personal freedom of wind and wave that only windsurfing can provide, we hope this book helps you to get the most out of the sport.

Chop jumping. As you take off, remember to sail the board through the air.

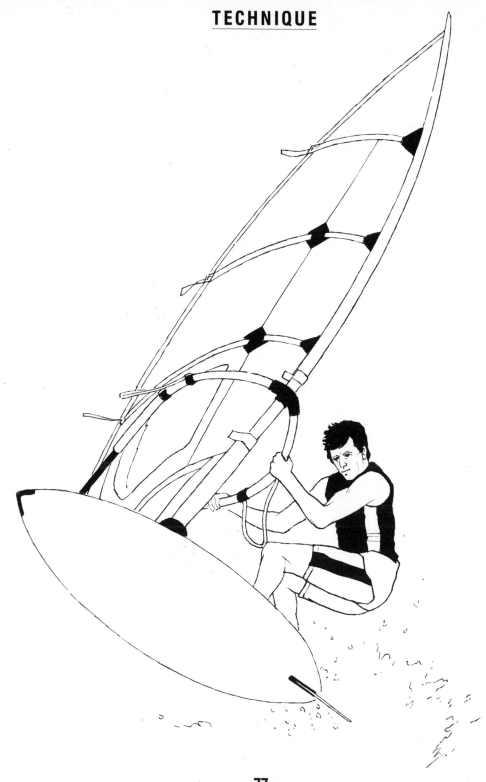

USEFUL
ADDRESSES

Royal Yachting Association
RYA House
Romsey Road
Eastleigh
Hants
SO5 4YA
Tel. 0703 629962

**Professional Boardsailing Association
(International)**
No. 1, Barn Cottages
Albany Park
Colnbrook
Slough
SL3 0HS
Tel. 0753 683484

United Kingdom Boardsailing Association
Masons Road
Stratford Upon Avon
Warwickshire
Tel. 0789 299574

British Windsurfing Association
86 Sinah Lane
Hayling Island
Hants
PO1 10JW
Tel. 0705 463595.

United States Boardsailing Association
P.O. Box 978
Hood River
OR 97031
Tel. 503-386-7440

**The author displays here the correct
upright stance while looking in the
direction of travel.**

INDEX

*Figures referred to in **bold** are photographs.*